WHITE HOUSE INSIDERS

What's It Like to Be the
FIRST LADY?

BY KATHLEEN CONNORS

Gareth Stevens
PUBLISHING

Please visit our website, www.garethstevens.com. For a free color catalog of all our high-quality books, call toll free 1-800-542-2595 or fax 1-877-542-2596.

Library of Congress Cataloging-in-Publication Data

Connors, Kathleen.
What's it like to be the First Lady? / by Kathleen Connors.
    p. cm. — (White House insiders)
Includes index.
ISBN 978-1-4824-1091-4 (pbk.)
ISBN 978-1-4824-1092-1 (6-pack)
ISBN 978-1-4824-1090-7 (library binding)
1. Presidents' spouses — United States — Juvenile literature. I. Connors, Kathleen. II. Title.
E176.2 C66 2015
973—d23

First Edition

Published in 2015 by
Gareth Stevens Publishing
111 East 14th Street, Suite 349
New York, NY 10003

Designer: Nick Domiano
Editor: Kristen Rajczak

Photo credits: cover, p. 1 (Michelle Obama) Jewel Samad/AFP/Getty Images; cover, p. 1 (Laura Bush) Joe Raedle/Getty Images News/Getty Images; cover, p. 1 (Jacqueline Kennedy) Art Rickerby/Time & Life Pictures/Getty Images; p. 5 John Parrot/Stocktrek Images/Getty Images; p. 7 Hulton Archive/Getty Images; p. 9 Francis Miller/Time & Life Pictures/Getty Images; p. 11 Diana Walker/Time & Life Pictures/Getty images; p. 13 David McNew/Hulton Archive/Getty Images; p. 15 Tim Sloan/AFP/Getty Images, p. 17 Theo Wargo/Getty Images Entertainment/Getty Images; p. 19 Win McNamee/Getty Images News/Getty Images.

Printed in the United States of America

CPSIA compliance information: Batch #CS15GS: For further information contact Gareth Stevens, New York, New York at 1-800-542-2595.

Glossary

Words in the glossary appear in **bold** type the first time they are used in the text.

Unofficial Role

In the US **Constitution**, the Founding Fathers outlined certain positions that needed to be filled in order for the government to run. The list includes the president, but there's no mention of the First Lady.

The First Lady is most often the president's wife, but nieces, sisters, daughters, and daughters-in-law have also stepped into the role. It's not an official government position, and there are no special duties given to the First Lady. This has allowed each First Lady to make the role her own.

The Inside Scoop

Historians say the title "First Lady" was first used in 1848 when President Zachary Taylor called Dolley Madison "the first lady of our land" at her funeral. By the late 1800s, "First Lady" was a widely used term.

Many First Ladies have looked to the example of past First Ladies, such as Martha Washington, to help shape their position.

5

Early On

The first First Ladies headed the president's household, oversaw the cleaning, and decorated. Each was expected to be a gracious hostess at dinners and parties.

By the early 1800s, the First Lady was already in the spotlight. What she wore, how often she entertained, and how she spent her free time were of great public interest. Early First Ladies, such as Dolley Madison, were often concerned with maintaining **prestige** without seeming too "queenly." They didn't want to seem too "common," either!

The Inside Scoop

Early First Ladies didn't want to be viewed as acting too "queenly" because most Americans still remembered living under the British **monarchy**.

Dolley Madison was praised as a hostess. She not only served as First Lady to her husband, President James Madison, but also hosted for President Thomas Jefferson before that. Jefferson's wife had died.

7

A Modern Lady

As women gained more rights and the United States grew in power, the First Lady's role changed. She began to **represent** the president and spoke out about **legislation** and causes she cared about.

That's not all that changed! Today, the First Lady lives at the White House—but she doesn't have to clean it. And while she still serves as a hostess at special dinners and events, the First Lady's schedule includes much more than parties.

The Inside Scoop

The First Lady's office is in the White House's East Wing. She can hire a staff of any size. Modern First Ladies commonly have at least a chief of staff, press secretary, director of special projects and **policy**, director of scheduling, and social secretary.

Eleanor Roosevelt proved the power of the First Lady as she took part in politics during and after her husband's time as president. She was First Lady for 12 years, from 1933 to 1945.

Giving Guidance

From the start, the First Lady was known as a close presidential adviser. Abigail Adams was even called "Mrs. President"! She often offered her opinions to her husband, John Adams, during his presidency from 1797 to 1801.

How much **influence** the First Lady's advice has changes with each new pair in office, though. Nancy Reagan kept President Reagan's schedule. In doing so, she might have been able to decide whom he met with and what events he attended. This could have had lasting political effects.

The Inside Scoop

While she was First Lady, Hillary Clinton won a court case that challenged her ability to hold closed meetings about political matters. The court acknowledged that presidents' wives have long acted as "advisers and personal representatives of their husbands."

It was said that Nancy Reagan "expanded the job of the First Lady into a sort of associate presidency."

A Cause of Her Own

The First Lady commonly has her own **agenda** to support along with that of the president. She will often host events and give speeches about a cause. Ellen Wilson, President Woodrow Wilson's first wife, worked to improve housing for the poor. She met with specialists and politicians about her concerns and eventually got a housing bill passed!

Other First Ladies have supported equal rights for women, education, and health care. Most continue to work for their cause after their time as First Lady ends.

The Inside Scoop

Many First Ladies have another role they take very seriously—mom! Anna Harrison had 10 children with her husband, President William Henry Harrison.

Between supporting the president's agenda and her own, the First Lady has a busy schedule! Here, Laura Bush reads to a group of children in a library.

13

Globetrotter

As the official US hostess, the First Lady often welcomes foreign leaders at the White House. She takes **diplomatic** trips with the president, too. Some of her travels are more political. In 1977, Rosalynn Carter traveled to Latin America and met with leaders about important matters, such as trade.

Today, it's common to hear of the First Lady traveling all over the world—and not just for political reasons. First Lady Michelle Obama, President Obama, and their two daughters vacationed in Hawaii in 2012.

The Inside Scoop

The First Lady doesn't get paid for any work she does. The government pays for her home, travel, and security, though.

Being in the public eye can be dangerous.
Just like the president, the First Lady has a
Secret Service team to protect her at all times.

15

Hillary Rodham Clinton

When campaigning for the presidency, Bill Clinton joked that the American people would be getting "two for the price of one"—he and his wife, Hillary Rodham Clinton. Hillary was a lawyer before becoming First Lady.

Hillary showed just how much influence a modern First Lady can gain. In 2001, she became a US Senator for New York. Then, she ran for president herself in 2008, eventually becoming secretary of state for President Barack Obama. What will she do next?

The Inside Scoop

As more women run for president, there could be a new role in the White House—the First Gentleman!

Hillary Clinton moved her office to the West Wing of the White House to be closer to the president, his staff, and all the political action! She led a committee on health care reform while her husband was president.

17

Michelle Obama

Michelle Obama took her job as First Lady seriously. In 2010, she started a campaign called Let's Move! to support healthier food in schools and to encourage children and families to exercise more. Michelle also worked to help soldiers and military families get any help they needed.

Michelle has said that there's more to her life than just being the First Lady. In 2009, she said, "I probably do just what your mom does every day. I spend my free time with my kids."

The Inside Scoop

Recent First Ladies have been just as educated as their husbands. Michelle Obama met President Barack Obama when they both worked as lawyers in Chicago, Illinois.

Michelle Obama has asked many celebrities to take part in her Let's Move! campaign, including Beyoncé and Shaquille O'Neal, shown here.

19

Life, Interrupted

First Ladies today are very busy—and often in the spotlight. Some find it hard to keep a sense of normalcy, especially with children. Michelle Obama has said she still goes to her daughters' sports games and has family dinners!

The First Ladies face comparisons, too. When asked what First Lady she was like, Laura Bush said, "I think I'll be Laura Bush." Her answer sums up the ever-changing role of First Lady, which is a job each woman shapes for herself and the needs of the country.

The Inside Scoop

It's common for the First Lady to redecorate parts of the White House when she moves in. Furthermore, she oversees decorating it for holidays!

Timeline

1789	Martha Washington becomes the first First Lady.
1844	Julia Tyler is the first photographed First Lady.
1850	Lucy Hayes graduates from college. She would be the first First Lady with a college degree.
1909–1913	Nellie Taft is the first First Lady to own and drive a car.
1921–1923	Florence Harding is the first First Lady to vote.
1961–1963	Jacqueline Kennedy is the first First Lady to hire a press secretary.
1969–1974	Pat Nixon is the first First Lady to wear pants in public.
1977–1981	Rosalynn Carter is the first First Lady to attend **Cabinet** meetings.
2008	Hillary Clinton is the first former First Lady to run for president.

Glossary

agenda: things someone wants to get done or talk about

Cabinet: the president's closest advisers

constitution: the basic laws by which a country or state is governed

diplomatic: having to do with diplomacy, or the art of guiding talks between nations

influence: to have an effect on

legislation: laws

monarchy: a government headed by a king or queen

policy: a plan of general and future decisions and positions

prestige: having importance in the eyes of the people

represent: to stand for

For More Information

BOOKS

Doak, Robin S. *Michelle Obama*. Chicago, IL: Capstone Raintree, 2014.

Raatma, Lucia. *First of the First Ladies: Martha Washington*. Minneapolis, MN: Compass Point Books, 2009.

WEBSITES

The First Ladies: The White House
www.whitehouse.gov/about/first-ladies
Learn about the lives of every First Lady in United States history.

National First Ladies' Library
www.firstladies.org
Plan a visit to this historic site, and find out about the many exciting exhibits.

Index